R.

Why Tradition-Why Now?

Brian Williams

As part of our commitment to beauty and the return of
reverence, Regina Press has issued this second edition
of *Liturgy Guy: Essays by Brian Williams* (re-titled and expanded)
at a reduced cost so that this message of liturgical restoration
may reach as wide of an audience as possible.

Published by Regina Press
A Division of Regina Foundation of Oregon

Regina Foundation of Oregon
12042 SE Sunnyside Road
Suite 486
Clackamas, Oregon 97015

ISBN-13: 978-0-9966479-2-2

Dedicated
to
the Women Responsible for this Book:

To Beverly, my publisher, who believed in this book
before I did.

To Aunt Nancy who, though not Catholic,
has read Liturgy Guy since day one.

To my mother Britt Marie,
who has told me since childhood I was a writer.

To my wonderful wife Angela,
who suggested I get off my soapbox and sit down at
my keyboard.

And to Our Lady, through whose intercession
and Most Holy Rosary I continue to grow in love
for
Our Lord, His Church, and the Holy Sacrifice of the
Mass.

ESSAYS

FORWARD

In the passing world, the almost transient world, of the
Internet, it is my opinion that the better blogs are the focused
ones, short and to the point. This even holds true for blogs
dealing with liturgy and Church life. With brevity and clarity,
they make their impact just as sound bites do elsewhere in the
news media. They can make your day, perhaps.

They might kick off a train of thought, but then they are gone.
I am glad Regina Press is publishing a second edition of the
collection of essays from Liturgy Guy. The cause of promoting
reverent worship and seeking the restoration of the
sacred needs fixed poles, the anchors that the print media can
surely provide.

I wish Brian Williams all the best with what is certainly a
valuable flanking maneuver to a noble cause. The recovery of
the sacred and a sense of the Divine Presence is the
cornerstone to a thoroughgoing renewal of Catholic life.

The Most Reverend Thomas E. Gullickson, JCD

Titular Archbishop of Bomarzo

Apostolic Nuncio in Switzerland and the Principality of

Liechtenstein

Bern, 29 September 2018

Feast of the Holy Archangels, Michael, Gabriel and Raphael

1. Why Tradition-
Why Now?

Disorder begets chaos, not peace.

In the years immediately following the Second Vatican Council Western Culture experienced rapid and widespread change.

Marriage and the family, the very foundation of society, were attacked at the core. No fault divorce, contraception, and eventually even abortion, found increasing acceptance within society.

For Catholics, however, there should have been stability, constancy. There was the Holy Mass. There was Catholic education.

There were priests and religious sisters forming and instructing. There was always the Catholic faith. Timeless, immutable, and transcendent.

There had been the Council. Announced by Pope John XXIII only a few months into his papacy, the Council would neither seek to declare dogma nor denounce heresy, but rather was only pastoral in its intent.

However, there were two great and ominous threats facing the Church. Threats that sought to destroy her, from within and from without: Modernism and Atheistic Communism.

Numerous popes, most notably St. Pius X, had warned against the Modernist heresy for nearly 100 years.

Bishop Fulton Sheen had warned a 1950's television audience of millions about the threat posed by Godless Communism.

Vatican II spoke not a single word against either.

In the decades since the close of the Council we have seen the Church become a devastated vineyard (to borrow Dietrich von Hildebrand's phrase). We have seen the widespread loss of sacrality in worship and in the family.

Disorder begets chaos, not peace.

The supreme prayer of the Church is the Holy Mass. It is, as St. Peter Julian Eymard called it, the "holiest act of religion." For nearly 1500 years the Roman Rite had gone largely unchanged. From ecclesial Latin, to the *Canon Missae*, to chant, all dated back to the time of St. Gregory the Great, if not older.

Centuries passed and the Mass continued to develop organically. The *Pater Noster*, the Last Gospel, even priestly vestments...additions and developments to the Roman liturgy. Not by meeting or committee, but slowly, over time, by local customs and faithful Catholics.

By 1970 disorder had become the norm. Chaos indeed followed. Instability and revolution molded modernity. What always was, was now questioned. Doubted. Clarity was for another era. A time past. Ambiguity was the preference of intellectuals and those who had no time for sacred mysteries and ancient rituals.

By 1970 the Mass of the Ages was gone. Not altogether, but nevertheless gone for all but a few of the faithful. At a time when storms raged and the ground shifted, the immutable and eternal...changed.

Literally, nothing was sacred anymore. What followed was largely a rush to the bottom, as the pedestrian and profane was extolled and the transcendent was escorted from the stage.

Disordered man brought chaos to the Mass:

● Ignoring all of Christian history, Catholics began to look at each other at Mass instead of God.

● Ignoring 17 centuries of tradition Catholics instead took their example from the western apostates and began to worship exclusively in the vernacular.

● Dismissing both the sacramental priesthood and the very Real Presence of Christ in the Eucharist, man began handling God himself, as if He were just mere bread, or as if we (the laity) had the consecrated hands of priests.

Gone was the Roman Canon, now just an option: Eucharistic Prayer 1.

Gone was Gregorian Chant, and this in spite of the liturgical movement.

Gone was the beauty of high altars, communion rails, and Catholic statuary. As we refused God our very best, denying Him truth, objective beauty and our very identity, the rest disappeared as well over time.

Catholic education largely waned. Gone were authentic parochial schools.

Religious orders slowly shriveled up, decimated by a post-conciliar culture that devalued contemplation, sacrifice, and discernment. Fewer religious meant fewer prayers and less grace. The world became less grace-filled.

Authenticity, the perennial means by which we evangelize, was lost the moment the Church sought to reinvent itself.

Amidst the ecclesial, cultural, and political chaos of the era the family often bore the brunt of the attack. The widespread acceptance of artificial birth control, the legalization of no fault divorce and eventually abortion, all took their toll.

Throw in feminism and its degradation of true femininity and the maternal nature, and the assault was complete.

A Church in flux and in self-doubt was no match. When peace and steadfastness were needed, the faithful were given chaos. When Catholics needed meat and potatoes and a fully caffeinated Catholicism, they were instead given rice cakes and decaf.

Tradition is that fully caffeinated Catholicism.

An increasing number of the faithful have discovered that we need tradition, and we need it now. We need order and peace. Restoring the sacred, returning to the Traditional Mass, is an intentional decision. It is fortification against disorder.

Tradition is an acknowledgement that the faith pre-dates the 1960s. It is the discovery that there is an entire language, and entirely different points of reference, when we immerse ourselves in the traditions of centuries. Not decades, but millennia.

Tradition is not nostalgia, nor is it a fad. It most certainly is not simply a preference either. It is finding the peace that comes from order, the order that comes from ritual, and the ritual that leads us to God.

Tradition is humility. It is deference to those who have come before us, and the obligation to those not yet born. It is the democracy of the dead, but also the future of the Church.

Tradition is restoration. It is the recovery of the sacred and an outright assault against disorder. It begins within the family, moves out to the parish community, then on to the diocese, the Church, the secular realm, and finally into the larger culture.

But it starts with the family. It is the principle of subsidiarity applied to prayer. It is the conscious decision to choose tradition.

We choose tradition.

2. Liturgical Game Changers

In his classic work *The Spirit of the Liturgy*, Joseph Cardinal Ratzinger references the Israelites' worship of the golden calf at Sinai as an example of man's inclination to profane worship:

The people cannot cope with the invisible, remote, and mysterious God. They want to bring him down into their own world, into what they can see and understand. Worship is no longer going up to God, but drawing God down into one's own world.

8

Understanding this, it is easy to see why certain liturgical practices - long associated with the traditional Mass and even the Reform of the Reform movement - are so widely opposed. In his post-conciliar zeal to desacralize the Holy Mass, man has no place for either mystery or the transcendent. Setting one's gaze upon God is antithetical to modern anthropocentric worship. This is also the reason why certain traditional practices are nothing less than liturgical 'game changers' when restored to the Mass.

These game changers are *ad orientem* worship, the use of Latin in the Liturgy, and the reception of Holy Communion on the tongue while kneeling.

The priest offering the Mass *ad orientem*, facing the altar (or tabernacle) instead of the people, is the first liturgical game changer. This, of course, was the historic manner in which the Church celebrated the Mass for nearly two millennia. As Fr. Joseph Fessio, S.J., of Ignatius Press noted:

It has been the practice in the entire Church, East and West from time immemorial. Contrary to a prevailing misconception (even among liturgists) there is no evidence for celebration of Mass coram populo (facing the people) in the first nineteen centuries of the Church's history, with rare exceptions. (Cf. The Spirit of the Liturgy, by

Cardinal Ratzinger, pp. 74-84.) The practice of reducing an altar to a table for a service facing the people began in the 16th century — with Martin Luther.

Only after having frequented Masses offered *ad orientem* can one truly grasp the relevance and theological richness of this traditional practice. As the entire community presents God with their prayers and offerings, priest and laity alike, it is only fitting that they approach Him together. In his book *Turning Towards the Lord*, Fr. Uwe Michael Lang writes:

The catch phrase often heard nowadays that the priest is 'turning his back on the people' is a classic example of confounding theology and topography, for the crucial point is that the Mass is a common act of worship where priest and people together, representing the pilgrim Church, reach out for the transcendent God.

The second game changer is the use of Latin in the Mass. This language of the liturgy has all but disappeared from the Roman Rite over the last five decades. In the weeks prior to the implementation of the Novus Ordo Mass in 1969, Pope Paul VI provided his reasoning for a largely vernacular Mass:

*Understanding of prayer is worth more than the
silken garments in which it is royally dressed.
Participation by the people is worth more -
particularly participation by modern people, so fond
of plain language which is easily understood and
converted into everyday speech.*

However, the near complete abandonment
of the traditional language of the Mass had
never been advocated for by Holy Mother
Church. Latin was always viewed as a
source of unity for the universal Church,
both across cultures and centuries. Less
than twenty years before the Second
Vatican Council, Pope Pius XII reminded
the faithful in his encyclical *Mediator Dei* that
the "...*use of the Latin language, customary in a
considerable portion of the Church, is a manifest and
beautiful sign of unity, as well as an effective
antidote for any corruption of doctrinal truth.*"

Even *Sacrosanctum Concilium*, the Second
Vatican Council's *Constitution on the Sacred
Liturgy*, reiterated the need for the faithful to
be able to say or sing the Ordinary of the
Mass in Latin.

In his address at the 2013 Sacra Liturgia
conference in Rome, Malcolm Cardinal
Ranjith explained how the use of Latin was
far more than just a matter of preference or
aesthetics:

The liturgical use of Latin in the Church, even though it starts somewhere in the fourth century A.D., gives rise to a series of expressions which are unique and which constitute the very faith of the Church. The vocabulary of the Credo is quite clearly filled with expressions in Latin which are untranslatable. The role of the lex orandi in determining the lex credendi of the Church is very much valid in the case of its use of Latin in the liturgy. For doctrine often evolves in the faith experience of prayer. For this reason, a healthy balance between the use of Latin and that of the vernacular languages should be maintained.

Of course, Latin represents a significant stumbling block for those who prefer a liturgy which seeks the horizontal over the vertical dimension. Because there is no room for personality or improvisation in a liturgy offered in a 'dead' language, it naturally thwarts those who view the Mass as an opportunity for self-expression and innovation. An anthropocentric liturgy cannot tolerate the use of Latin as it prevents the community from celebrating itself.

Additionally, the use of Latin further highlights that the Mass is a sacrifice offered to God. Indeed, it is our participation in the Sacrifice of Calvary, and not simply a communion meal as commemorated by

Protestants. This emphasis on the Sacrifice of the Mass is something largely rejected by those 'ecumaniacs' (as Cardinal Heenan called them) who have sought for decades to 'Protestantize' the Catholic Mass.

The third and final liturgical game changer is the reception by the faithful of communion on the tongue while kneeling. Nothing speaks more clearly to our belief in the Real Presence than the manner in which we receive Our Lord during Holy Communion. The traditional practice of receiving the Eucharist on the tongue and while kneeling is one of humility and reverence. This public and liturgical affirmation of our belief in the Eucharist is the most counter-cultural thing we do each week. It is the ultimate "Amen!" ...the physical manifestation of "I do believe!"

In *Dominus Es t - It is the Lord*, Bishop Athanasius Schneider explains the power behind this manner of receiving:

Allowing oneself to be fed like a baby by receiving Communion directly into the mouth ritually expresses in a better way the character of receptivity and of being a child before Christ Who feeds us and nourishes us spiritually.

This of course makes it perfectly clear as to why this is such a game changer. How many

Catholics today have the humility to be fed
the Body of Christ? How many today truly
believe that it is the Lord who they are
being asked to kneel before? Restoring the
traditional practice compels the faithful to
demonstrate what it is we profess: that this
Eucharist is not just ordinary bread.
Lukewarm Catholics will not kneel and be
fed.

In October 1966, noted Catholic theologian
Dietrich von Hildebrand wrote, "The new
liturgy actually threatens to frustrate the
confrontation with Christ, for it discourages
reverence in the face of mystery, precludes
awe, and all but extinguishes a sense of
sacredness."

For fifty years the faithful have seen a sense
of the sacred extinguished in their parishes
through liturgical innovation. It is my hope
and my prayer that these liturgical game
changers would receive further attention.

May that generation of priests and pastors
who came of age during the papacy of
Benedict XVI seek to implement these
practices, and in so doing, better aid the
faithful to soar up and encounter God in the
Holy Mass.

3. Why Aren't More Masses Offered *Ad Orientem*?

This was the question that I recently posed to several priests: Why aren't more Masses being offered *ad orientem*? As we have seen numerous books and articles in recent years convincingly argue for a return to *ad orientem* worship, it is unfortunate to see how few priests have actually returned to the traditional orientation. Despite well received scholarly works by Monsignor Klaus Gamber, Fr. Uwe Michael Lang, and Joseph Cardinal Ratzinger arguing in favor of it, few Catholics ever see the Novus Ordo offered *ad orientem*, with the notable exceptions of two dioceses: Arlington, Virginia and Lincoln, Nebraska.

Discussing the topic with several diocesan priests, an explanation for the continuing reluctance to offer the Mass *ad orientem* can be broken out into five categories:

1. There are still priests who incorrectly believe that the Novus Ordo should only be offered *versus populum* (facing the people); often this is argued by referencing the General Instruction of the Roman Missal (GIRM) #299. There are also priests who, while understanding that the Mass can be offered *ad orientem*, believe that the 'spirit' of the modern liturgy argues against it. As one priest reminded me, the quality of seminary formation (as it relates to the liturgy) has been quite poor for decades.

2. Some priests truly think that facing the people is a good thing. They contend that it brings people closer to the Mass because it lets people see what is 'going on'. Unfortunately, there are many who have likely accepted the false narrative that offering the Mass *ad orientem*

amounts to the priest 'turning his back'.

3. At the same time, there are priests who tend to be conservative regarding faith and morals, but who are either uneducated on the subject or simply disinterested in matters regarding the sacred liturgy. While these priests will try their best to offer a reverent Novus Ordo, 'hot button' topics such as the use of Latin, Gregorian chant, Communion on the tongue and *ad orientem* are either ignored or viewed as unimportant.

4. Then there are the true 'progressives' who have welcomed these changes to the Church's worship, and who now hope to see doctrinal changes too (lex orandi, lex credendi).

5. Finally, there are priests, often ordained in the last ten years and with some exposure to the Latin Mass, who would offer more Masses *ad orientem* but are simply afraid to. Some fear the reactions of their parishioners; some that of their brother priests; most often, however, it is their bishop who they fear. Sadly, there are still dioceses where

any semblance of liturgical
'traditionalism' is strictly verboten.

In the short-term there will be no
widespread change, no return to the historic
liturgical orientation of the Mass, without it
being mandated either by Rome or the
USCCB. Of course, no one expects this to
happen. Unfortunately, regardless of what
Robert Cardinal Sarah might say in
interviews (in his capacity as Prefect for the
Congregation for Divine Worship), or the
liturgical examples given by both Pope
Benedict and Pope Francis on several
occasions, nothing short of a mandate
changes the current environment.

So, are those of us who recognize the
theological and liturgical importance of this
matter simply left to despair? Thankfully,
the answer is no. What we can do now is to
continue encouraging our priests and
bishops who know the significance of
liturgical orientation to renew their effort to
reform the rite.

In the past, I have written about liturgical
game changers as well as those elements of
the Liturgy which help to restore a sense of
the sacred. It is interesting to note that, as
far as the faithful are concerned, this matter
of ad orientem worship might be the easiest
change to implement.

Several priests I spoke with said that integrating more Latin into the Novus Ordo Mass, or reintroducing traditional hymns (or sung Propers) to their parishes was a much greater source of conflict. In many places, parishioners are more vested in their Seventies folk hymns and Haugen and Haas music than the direction of the priest during the Mass. Likewise, the reintroduction of Latin has at times resulted in greater pushback, as many Catholics incorrectly view the Novus Ordo as the 'vernacular only' Mass (an idea declared anathema by the Council of Trent).

Priests who already offer the Mass ad orientem told me that the faithful by and large accepted the change following targeted catechesis, both through homilies and bulletin inserts. This isn't to say that some parishioners didn't leave; rather that their departure was offset by the arrival of new families intentionally seeking the sacred. In addition, the change was at times preceded by a return to male only altar servers, kneelers brought out for Holy Communion, and a general overall return of reverence. In some cases, the introduction of *ad orientem* was made during an abbreviated liturgical season such as Lent or Advent, and often with daily Masses at first.

So much of Pope Benedict's papacy was directed toward implementing authentic reform and renewal versus the discontinuity and rupture so widespread in the decades following the Council. In the liturgy of the Roman Rite there may be no greater visual representation of discontinuity than the near universal abandonment of *ad orientem* Masses in the Novus Ordo. Conversely, there may be no better way to immediately begin restoring a sense of liturgical continuity than for the priest to once again face the liturgical East together with the faithful. Let us dare hope that, as more holy priests and bishops take this into consideration, we might begin to see more Masses offered *ad orientem*.

4. Seven Reasons for the Use of Latin in the Mass

There have been few topics of discussion as contentious in the post-Conciliar years as the use of Latin within the Mass. The near universal disappearance of Latin from the liturgical life of the Church has been one of the great casualties of the 'spirit of Vatican II'. It is my hope that these reasons will lead some to reassess their bias against the use of Latin in the Mass. Much of what is written below comes directly from *The Catechism Explained: An Exhaustive Explanation of the Catholic Religion* by Father Francis Spirago.

Seven Reasons for the Use of Latin in the Mass

1. The Latin language is venerable on account of its origin and its antiquity; indeed, it dates to the earliest centuries of the Church and to the very Masses offered in the obscurity of the Catacombs.

2. There is an element of mystery about Latin. It is a dead language, not spoken by the faithful. The use of Latin conveys to the mind of the people that something is going on upon the altar which is beyond their comprehension; that a mystery is being enacted.

3. Latin is a liturgical language for Catholics. It is a striking fact that both Jews and pagans made use, in their worship of the Deity, of a language with which the multitudes were not conversant. The Jews in fact made use of Hebrew, the language of the patriarchs; we do not see Our Lord or the apostles censuring this practice.

4. The use of Latin in the Mass is a means of maintaining unity in the Catholic Church, for the use of one and the same language in Latin Rite

churches all over the world is a connecting link to Rome, as well as between nations separated by their cultures and native tongues.

5. Latin is a safeguard against error because of its immutability. The near exclusive use of the vernacular inevitably leads to heresies and errors creeping into the Church. Likewise, the use of Latin helps to define and defend orthodoxy. As noted by Malcolm Cardinal Ranjith at Sacra Liturgia (2013):

The liturgical use of Latin in the Church...gives rise to a series of expressions which are unique and which constitute the very faith of the Church. The vocabulary of the Credo is quite clearly filled with expressions in Latin which are untranslatable. The role of the lex orandi in determining the lex credendi of the Church is very much valid in the case of its use of Latin in the liturgy. For doctrine often evolves in the faith experience of prayer...

6. It is unnecessary for the faithful to hear, or understand, every ceremonial of the Mass. History has clearly shown, and experience teaches, that the fact of the prayers being in Latin does not at all hamper or interfere with the devotion of the faithful, or lead them to absent

themselves from Holy Mass. As Saint Augustine instructed: "If there are some present who do not understand what is being said or sung, they know at least that all is said and sung to the glory of God, and that is sufficient for them to join in it devoutly."

7. The primary reason why the whole of the Mass was historically offered in Latin is because it is a sacrifice, not an instruction for the people. The celebration of Mass consists more in action than in words. This final reason cannot be overstated. A Protestant gathering which commemorates the Lord's Supper is simply a service of prayers and instruction. For this reason, the vernacular is a necessity. The Catholic Mass, however, is a holy sacrifice offered to God the Father by an ordained priest, in persona Christi. The action of the Mass, and the mystery of it, is reinforced by the use of Latin.

In his 1962 apostolic constitution *Veterum Sapientia*, Pope St. John XXIII observed that:

The Catholic Church has a dignity far surpassing that of every merely human society, for it was founded by Christ the Lord. It is altogether fitting, therefore, that the language it uses should be noble, majestic, and non-vernacular.

May more priests and bishops in the coming years recognize that the use of Latin should not simply be limited to Masses offered in the Extraordinary Form. Indeed, both forms of the Roman Rite have every reason to be celebrated in a language that is 'noble, majestic, and non-vernacular.'

5. The Affirmative Argument for Receiving Communion on the Tongue

A recent post at the website *Roman Catholic Man* has focused a great deal of attention on the manner in which the faithful receive Communion. As any discussion regarding the Eucharist is a discussion about Our Lord Himself, the importance of this topic cannot be overstated. Bishop Athanasius Schneider recently noted that we are experiencing the fourth great crisis in the history of the

Church, and our casual and 'banal treatment of the Eucharist is the greatest sign of the crisis.'

Now is indeed the time to revisit the topic. Putting aside opinions and personal preferences, let us objectively discuss this matter of paramount importance. Unfortunately, all too often it is viewed as the third rail of liturgical discussions. But it need not be this way.

The argument in favor of the traditional practice of receiving Communion on the tongue is indeed an affirmative one: For over a thousand years the Faithful of the Roman Rite only received Communion on the tongue while kneeling.

It is true that some communities in the early Church received the Eucharist in the hand; however, the universal practice of only receiving Communion on the tongue is evident by the eighth century and remained until the 1970s.

Indults permitting Communion in the hand were an innovation of the Seventies to accommodate those countries who had already initiated the practice illicitly.

The majority of Eastern Rite churches have never permitted the faithful to receive in the hand. For that matter, the Extraordinary Form of the Mass in the Roman rite also does not permit reception in the hand.

Rome has continuously instructed the faithful on the merit and universality of the traditional practice for as long as the indults have been in place. As recently as 2008, the Office for the Liturgical Celebrations of the Supreme Pontiff stated:

From the time of the Fathers of the Church, a tendency was born and consolidated whereby distribution of Holy Communion in the hand became more and more restricted in favor of distributing Holy Communion on the tongue. The motivation for this practice is two-fold: a) first, to avoid, as much as possible, the dropping of Eucharistic particles; b) second, to increase among the faithful devotion to the Real Presence of Christ in the Sacrament of the Eucharist.

Belief in the Real Presence has steadily decreased for forty years as the posture of kneeling has been lost. In his seminal work *The Spirit of the Liturgy*, Cardinal Joseph Ratzinger prophetically noted that "...the man who learns to believe learns also to kneel, and a faith or a liturgy no longer familiar with kneeling would be sick at the core. Where it has been lost, kneeling must be rediscovered... (p. 194)."

Brian Williams

Thankfully, the faithful need not wait for the indults to be lifted to recapture this venerable practice. Holy Mother Church has given her children ample instruction on the matter. Pope Benedict provided us extensive catechesis on this subject, most particularly by his personal example at papal Masses.

Clergy need not wait either. There are parishes today reinstalling communion rails in order to recapture this sacred tradition. Others are simply bringing in kneelers for the faithful to use during Mass in order to recover this posture of reverence and adoration.

Cardinal Antonio Canazares Llovera, when he was Prefect of the Congregation for Divine Worship and the Discipline of the Sacraments, said it best when he noted that receiving on the tongue while kneeling "...is the sign of adoration that needs to be recovered (by the Church) ...we cannot lose a moment as important as that of Communion, of recognizing the real presence of Christ there."

29

6. The All Too Ordinary Use of Extraordinary Ministers

Many Catholic faithful over the last forty years have seen the all too common utilization of Extraordinary Ministers of Holy Communion during the Mass. An innovation from the 1970s intended for occasional use in emergency situations, these Extraordinary Ministers have indeed become quite ordinary in your ordinary parish Mass on any given Sunday. Sadly, this modern practice has contributed greatly to the blurring of lines between the sanctuary and the nave, as well as between the ordained and the laity.

The Original Intent

In January, 1973, the Sacred Congregation of the Sacraments (now called the Congregation for Divine Worship and the Discipline of the Sacraments) issued the document *Immensae Caritatis*, which established Special Ministers of the Eucharist to assist with distribution of Holy Communion, particular at Masses when other priests or deacons were not available, when either ill-health or old age impeded the celebrant from distributing communion alone, or most notably, whenever the number of faithful wishing to receive communion was so great that the Mass would take too long. How is that for an arbitrary standard?

What has of course happened in the ensuing decades since this provision was made is a long history of liturgical excesses and abuses. As is often the case, the exception has now become the norm.

The most obvious abuse that we have all witnessed is the sheer number of Extraordinary Ministers of Holy Communion typically used at any given Mass. A liturgical exception meant to be reserved for special emergency situations has become standard operating procedure in far too many parishes.

To address this ongoing problem, in August 1997 the Vatican issued the instruction *On Certain Questions Regarding the Collaboration of the Non-Ordained Faithful in the Sacred Ministry of Priest.* In Section 2 Article 8 the Church once again clarified that the use of these Extraordinary Ministers should only be utilized "...where there are particularly large numbers of the faithful and which (the Mass) would be excessively prolonged because of an insufficient number of ordained ministers to distribute Holy Communion."

In addition, the Church stressed the avoidance and elimination of certain practices which had emerged in certain dioceses and parishes and were creating confusion. One such practice? The habitual use of Extraordinary Ministers of Holy Communion at Mass thus arbitrarily extending the concept of 'a great number of the faithful.'

There is an immediate way to reduce this abuse of the current practice, an approach that has already been implemented in some parishes and which reduces the need for many of these Extraordinary Ministers: stop distributing Holy Communion under both kinds at Mass.

Brian Williams

The Doctrine of Concomitance

If more parishes chose to return to the traditional practice of distributing only the consecrated host to the faithful at Mass we would immediately remove the need for half of the Extraordinary Ministers currently assisting at communion.

For over a millennium the Latin Rite of the Catholic Church did not offer the chalice to the faithful. The Doctrine of Concomitance, the belief of our Lord's entire presence in either element of the Eucharist (bread or wine), was reaffirmed at the Council of Trent when the Church declared: "If anyone denies that Christ, the fountain and author of all graces, is received whole and entire under the one species of bread...let him be anathema. (Session XXI, Canon III)"

If we the faithful receive our Lord entirely (body, blood, soul and divinity) when we receive the consecrated host, then why is it necessary to stand in line for an Extraordinary Minister to give us our Lord entirely (again) in the chalice? The Church further stated at Trent that "...those who receive one species only are not deprived of any grace necessary to salvation." That being the case, why do so many parishes unnecessarily create a need for Extraordinary Ministers by offering

Communion under both kinds at every Sunday Mass?

Liturgical Consistency

A common theme I often write about is the need to reestablish consistency between the two forms of the Roman Rite, as well as recovering continuity with our liturgical heritage. Many parishes are already incorporating this approach. Since the Traditional Latin Mass does not permit for either the use of Extraordinary Ministers of Holy Communion or the offering of the chalice to the faithful at Communion, the implementation of this suggested reform would create further visible consistency between the two forms of the Mass.

In our continuing effort to restore a sense of the sacred to the liturgy, let us pray that this ordinary use of Extraordinary Ministers soon becomes a thing of the past.

7. Altar Rails and Reverence

Altar rails are making a comeback and with their return so is reverence. It is becoming more common these days to see the installation of rails as an integral component of liturgical reform and church architecture. From dioceses as diverse as Charlotte, North Carolina, to Madison, Wisconsin, the rail has returned.

To be clear, there was never a requirement to remove altar rails (also called communion rails) in the years following the Second Vatican Council. However, there were many in the Church who aggressively sought to remove that which was considered traditional and sacred. Gone were the high altars, beautiful Catholic statuary, and of course, altar rails.

A liturgically misguided attempt at egalitarianism ruled the post-conciliar landscape, one which challenged the very distinction between sanctuary and nave. Overtones of anticlericalism were pervasive, as was a new type of Catholic worship, one intentionally structured for ecumenical purposes.

By their very presence altar rails hindered the march toward the profane desired by many. With such liturgical innovations as Extraordinary Ministers of Holy Communion and most particularly the practice of Communion in the hand, altar rails were an affront to the moderns. In the new, democratic, liturgy kneeling had simply become outdated and uncouth.

In his seminal work *The Spirit of the Liturgy*, Cardinal Ratzinger noted that, "The man who learns to believe learns also to kneel, and a faith or a liturgy no longer familiar with kneeling would be sick at the core." In recent years, however, there has been a slow yet steady healing occurring within the liturgy.

Church designers, architects and historians such as Duncan Stroik and Denis

McNamara have done their part in this effort. McNamara, who is a professor at the Liturgical Institute of the University of Saint Mary of the Lake in Mundelein, addressed the theological significance of rails in a July 2011 interview with the National Catholic Register:

[The altar rail] is still a marker of the place where heaven and earth meet, indicating that they are not yet completely united...But, at the same time, the rail is low, very permeable, and has a gate, so it does not prevent us from participating in heaven. So, we could say there is a theology of the rail, one which sees it as more than a fence, but as a marker where heaven and earth meet, where the priest, acting in persona Christi, reaches across from heaven to earth to give the Eucharist as the gift of divine life.

Altar rails are contributing to the restoration of the sacred and the recovery of reverence within the Holy Mass. At my home parish of St. Ann's in Charlotte, North Carolina, the rail returned with the 2009 renovation of the church. The altar rail was installed to accommodate the Traditional Latin Mass which was offered weekly. Over time the use of the rail was expanded to include all Masses, whether offered in the Ordinary Form or Extraordinary Form.

The altar rail has also returned to Sacred Heart Catholic Church in Salisbury, North

Carolina, (also in the Diocese of Charlotte).
While the new church was completed back
in 2009, the rail was not installed until just
last year in support of the weekly Sunday
Traditional Latin Mass.

More recently there is also the story of St.
Mary's of Pine Bluff, Wisconsin. Father
Richard Heilman, pastor, had the altar rail
installed earlier this year following a
$20,000 gift from an anonymous donor.
Overall the return of the rail has been well
received by his parishioners. Since Fr.
Heilman was already offering the Mass *ad
orientem*, and using kneelers for the faithful
at Holy Communion, the reintroduction of
the altar rail made perfect sense. More
importantly, Father has seen reverence for
the Eucharist continue to grow. Much like
St. Ann's in Charlotte, the majority of
parishioners at St. Mary's of Pine Bluff
choose to receive Communion on the
tongue.

It is fitting to conclude with the words of
our pope emeritus, Benedict XVI, when he
was still Cardinal Ratzinger, Prefect of the
Congregation for the Doctrine of the Faith.
Ratzinger noted that

*...the practice of kneeling for Holy Communion has
in its favor a centuries-old tradition, and it is a
particularly expressive sign of adoration, completely*

appropriate in light of the true, real and substantial presence of Our Lord Jesus Christ under the consecrated species.

Pray that more Catholics are blessed to experience the return of the altar rail to their parish and to receive Holy Communion while kneeling.

8. Altar Serving Seen Through Secular Eyes

There is no quicker way to get labeled a misogynist today than to suggest an end to girls serving at the altar. If you doubt the validity of that claim, try writing a blog post or two on the topic and see what happens.

Sadly, those who most often speak out in support of the current practice do so with little more than feelings and personal anecdotes.

When revisiting this topic, it is still surprising to see just how entrenched many are in their support of female servers. While it was the revision to canon law in 1983 that opened the door for girls to serve, official permission did not come from Rome until 1994.

Consider that for a moment.
For a Church that is 2,000 years old, the practice of girls serving at the altar is not even as old as Justin Bieber. And yet it is defended as if there is no questioning the practice, no turning back, no need to revisit something that was immediately adopted by almost every diocese in the United States without any deliberation.

It is important to remember what the Congregation for Divine Worship clearly said in 1994 regarding the connection between serving and vocations:

The Holy See wishes to recall that it will always be very appropriate to follow the noble tradition of having boys serve at the altar. As is well known, this has led to a reassuring development of priestly vocations. Thus the obligation to support such groups of altar boys will always continue.

Writing on this very topic over at his blog, Fr. John Zuhlsdorf methodically explained the change this way:

1. Diocesan Bishops can choose to authorize, or not, service at the altar by females.

2. Just because another diocese has service by women, that does not mean any other diocese has to have it.

3. Priests cannot be forced to have females serve their Masses.

4. Pastors cannot be forced by bishops to have female servers.

5. There is an obligation to support the service at the altar by boys.

6. There is a connection between service at the altar by boys and vocations to the priesthood.

7. No lay person has the right to serve at the altar for Mass or any other liturgical worship.

Unfortunately, pervasive secular understandings of equality and participation are repeatedly interjected into any discussion of altar girls. The contemporary belief that participation at Mass absolutely mandates the 'doing' of something has often resulted in the push for girls to serve.

Some cannot comprehend the notion that young women would actually be excluded from an activity that their brothers are allowed to do. They contend that girls can do anything the boys can do...and often better, a straw-man argument since no one is disputing this.

The question is asked: Why would we want to tell these young women that their service is not appreciated or wanted? After all, what about their feelings? Aren't we just bullying these young girls who want simply to serve Our Lord by serving at Mass?

As a father of five children, four of whom are girls, I soundly reject the idea that it is unfair to only permit boys to serve. To make this a false issue of 'rights' or to suggest that a girl's value can only be found by fulfilling the traditional role of a boy is wrong. However, as catechesis has suffered for decades, many Catholics can only see the faith through secular eyes.

Lost on many of the faithful is the understanding that society's idea of equality, one that no longer even acknowledges the difference between a man and a woman, has no place in the realm of the sacred. After all, if the majority of self-identified Catholics in the U.S. support female ordination and same-sex marriage (and they do), then how can we expect them to understand that the dignity of an individual does not depend upon the 'sameness' of everyone's roles?

Newsflash: boys and girls are different. That is a good thing. This understanding of our unique differences, our different purposes, actually helps to reinforce the Church's correct (but counter-cultural) understanding of the complementarity of the sexes.

While those who most vocally endorse altar girls say they oppose the call for female ordination, it is interesting to note the growing support for it over recent years. Common sense suggests that as more of the faithful argue that girls are "just as capable as the boys" to serve at mass, many will then go on to argue that women are "just as capable as men" of celebrating the Mass.

The theological, historical and scriptural arguments against it are undoubtedly lost on those who have been far more formed by the secular culture than by the Church.

A little over a decade ago the Gallup organization noted: "In 1977, only 36% of Catholic respondents agreed that it was a good thing for women to be ordained as priests. By the year 2000, 68% said they favored allowing women to become members of the clergy. A Quinnipiac University survey in October 2013 reported similar results with 66% of occasional mass attendees supporting female ordination.

It was no coincidence that Saint John Paul II released his Apostolic Letter *Ordinatio Sacerdotalis* in May 1994, only two months after the Congregation for Divine Worship released their letter permitting altar girls. St. John Paul II wrote:

Wherefore, in order that all doubt may be removed regarding a matter of great importance, a matter which pertains to the Church's divine constitution itself, in virtue of my ministry of confirming the brethren (cf. Lk 22:32) I declare that the Church has no authority whatsoever to confer priestly ordination on women and that this judgment is to be definitively held by all the Church's faithful.

Another argument often made is that "Rome has already spoken" on this subject and that the popes have consistently demonstrated their support for the use of altar girls. In other words, if it is allowed, what more is there to discuss? Of course, this confuses what is allowed with what is best.

For example, if one finds that priestly vocations are impacted by girls serving, is it not worth revisiting? Some argue that the available data on the topic of serving and vocations does not prove causation, but rather, correlation at best. So be it.

What we do know is that between 70-80% of the men ordained to the priesthood over the past five years share the common experience of altar serving in their youth. We also know from data collected on female religious professing their perpetual vows the last three years that only 10-15% were ever altar servers.

No doubt more conclusive data is needed as many other factors come into play. Having said this, it seems that those who support the modern practice of altar girls the most have little interest in research; most of all the USCCB. It boggles the mind that our bishops will not study this issue despite its implications for priestly vocations. It is the third rail of Catholicism.

In the end, this is the real reason why this conversation is so difficult to have. For many in the Church today it is easier to embrace the politically correct and politically expedient position. This, coupled with an infusion of modern, secular sensibilities regarding ideas such as participation and equality, means that altar serving will be a contentious topic for many years to come.

9. Busting the Myth of Altar Girls and Female Vocations

In the past, my posts on the correlation between altar boys and increased vocations to the priesthood have generated quite a bit of discussion. At times those who most vocally support the modern practice of girls serving express little concern over its potential detriment to priestly vocations. Proponents often assume that altar serving impacts female discernment in a manner very similar to that of men's.

But is this really the case? And ultimately, is it even relevant to a discussion about altar serving?

The most recent CARA study of men and women religious making their perpetual vows in 2015 reported only 20% of women having ever served altar. Compare this to teaching faith formation (48%) and singing in choir (33%), and you can see that altar serving impacts female discernment much less than other ministries.

Women surveyed by CARA in 2013 and 2012 responded in a similar manner. In both years only 15% of those making their perpetual vows had ever been altar servers. Religious education, music, and social service ministries were all much more common formative experiences among the women surveyed each year.

Likewise, we can contrast this with men ordained to the priesthood each of the last five years, where we see between 70-80% having served at the altar. Of course, this only makes sense as the altar boy is an extension of the liturgical function of the priest, something that inevitably contributes to the ongoing process of discernment through involvement.

Now think about this: The Italian slang word for altar boy is chierichetto, which means little clergymen. That about says it all.

We need not make this more complicated than it is. Vocations boom now just as they did in the past, where Catholicism is authentic, and where truth, beauty and goodness are demonstrated. This tends to be where the sacred is winning over the secular.

Girls will continue to discern their vocation, either to marriage or to the consecrated life, the same way as they have for centuries, when marriage and female orders flourished: through personal piety and through authentic role models.

If you want to help young women discern their vocation, increase their exposure to thriving, orthodox, female religious orders, and not by involving them in a liturgical role intended to foster vocations to the male only priesthood.

10. Busting the Myth of the Tridentine Mass

Far too often these days liturgical discussions pertaining to the Roman Rite start with the popular myth that the Traditional Latin Mass *only* dates back to the sixteenth century and the Council of Trent (1545-1563). While some make this claim simply due to a lack of catechesis, there are unfortunately others who perpetuate the myth to diminish the very antiquity of the ancient rite. Let us remedy this by busting the myth of the "Tridentine" Mass.

First a note on terminology. The Tridentine Mass is simply another name for the Traditional Latin Mass, also called the Extraordinary Form of the

Roman Rite since *Summorum Pontificum* was issued by Pope Benedict XVI in 2007.

Now for the history. Following the Council of Trent, Pope St. Pius V issued the papal Bull *Quo Primum* regarding the Mass. It is important to note that Pius V did not invent a new Mass (as Paul VI did in 1970), but rather consolidated and codified the Roman Rite already in existence. He also extended its use throughout the Latin Church, granting exception only to those rites demonstrating continuous usage of more than 200 years, such as the Ambrosian Rite found in Milan.

Since the 1570 Missal of Pius V was issued in the wake of the Council of Trent, the ancient rite has often been referred to as the Tridentine Mass. While there is nothing inherently wrong with this term, it can (and has) been used by some seeking to diminish the ancient rite by implying that it *only* dates back to 1570.

This, of course, is a myth.

Writing 50 years before the Second Vatican Council (1962-1965) and the promulgation of the new Mass of Paul VI (1970), Father Adrian Fortescue discussed the very antiquity of the Roman Rite in his classic, *The Mass: A Study of the Roman Liturgy (1912)*:

> Essentially the Missal of St. Pius V is the Gregorian Sacramentary; that again is

formed from the Gelasian book which depends on the Leonine collection. We find the prayers of our Canon in the treatise *de Sacramentis* and allusions to it in the IV century. So our Mass goes back, without essential change, to the age when it first developed out of the oldest liturgy of all. It is still redolent of that liturgy, of the days when Caesar ruled the world and thought he could stamp out the faith of Christ, when our fathers met together before dawn and sang a hymn to Christ as to a God. The final result of our enquiry is that, in spite of unsolved problems, in spite of later changes, there is not in Christendom another rite so venerable as ours.

And this of course is the point. Not that the Mass didn't develop organically, because it had. Nor that there were no further revisions to it, since the Missal of 1962 used in the Extraordinary Form today incorporates (as one example) the Holy Week revisions of 1955. But rather, that the Traditional Mass dates back to the oldest liturgy of all "without essential change", to use Fr. Fortescue's phrase. When referencing this Mass, we are speaking in terms of millennia, not centuries.

Indeed, some have referred to the traditional liturgy as the Gregorian Rite, or the Gregorian Mass, in deference to the ancient sacramentary bearing the name of that sixth century saint; a pope and liturgy which preceded Trent by one thousand years.

As liturgical discussions move forward within the Church, and both forms of the Roman Rite are studied and considered, let us hope that (at a minimum) we can finally bust the myth that the Traditional Mass is a product of the 16th century. If we are truly to restore all that has been lost for so many, we must first begin with correct information and intellectual honesty.

11. Western Civilization Exists for the Mass

Many are stunned today at the speed in which western civilization is collapsing. Coinciding with this is the post-conciliar crisis within the Church, the fourth great crisis of Christendom as it has been described by that great defender of orthodoxy, Bishop Athanasius Schneider of Kazakhstan. What may not be as clear too many is the connection between the destruction of the Mass and of the collapse of the Christian west.

One man who understood this connection was Dr. John Senior, professor of English, Literature, and Classics and co-founder of the very successful Integrated Humanities Program at the University of Kansas. Dr. Senior taught for decades at the university level. He was also a convert to the

Catholic faith, devoted to the traditional Mass and an attendee of Immaculata Chapel (SSPX) in St. Mary's, Kansas.

Senior has been credited with inspiring a generation of young men and women who, having studied under him at Kansas, converted to Catholicism. As Michael Matt of the Remnant has noted, "under his tutelage, (his students) had learned to love the old Faith as he did and thus desired to serve the Church as loyally as had their revered teacher."

Early in his book The Restoration of Christian Culture, John Senior speaks to the inseparable nature of civilization and the Holy Sacrifice of the Mass:

> Whatever we do in the political or social order, the indispensable foundation is prayer, the heart of which is the Holy Sacrifice of the Mass, the perfect prayer of Christ Himself, Priest and Victim, recreating in an unbloody manner the bloody, selfsame Sacrifice of Calvary. What is Christian culture? It is essentially the Mass. That is not my or anyone's opinion or theory or wish but the central fact of 2,000 years of history. Christendom, what secularists call Western Civilization, is the Mass and the paraphernalia which protect and facilitate it. All architecture, art, political and social forms, economics, the way people live and feel and think, music, literature —all these things when they are

> *right are ways of fostering and protecting the Holy*
> *Sacrifice of the Mass.*

Understanding this, is it any wonder why a growing number of Catholics today (sometimes derisively dismissed as 'radical traditionalists') speak of the need for liturgical restoration? Is it any surprise that we are seeing a cultural collapse in the west considering the anthropocentric and profane Masses offered for much of the last fifty years?

Reading the above quote by Senior recently I was immediately reminded of another occasion when esteemed laity highlighted the inseparable connection between the Mass and civilization.

On the eve of the implementation of Pope Paul's new Mass in the U.K. back in 1971, a group of learned English signatories wrote the Holy Father a letter, an appeal. Many of the distinguished signers were not even Catholic. They included such artists and thinkers as Agatha Christie, Graham Greene, Robert Graves, Ralph Richardson, Kenneth Clark, Malcolm Muggeridge, and Yehudi Menuhin to name just a few. In total nearly sixty people signed.

Their letter today, and the subsequent response of Rome, are referred to as the Agatha Christie indult, named after its most prominent signer. Put simply, the letter argued for the preservation of the Roman Rite as the jewel of western civilization. They began:

> *If some senseless decree were to order the total or partial destruction of basilicas or cathedrals, then obviously it would be the educated ~whatever their personal beliefs~ who would rise up in horror to oppose such a possibility.*

> *Now the fact is that basilicas and cathedrals were built so as to celebrate a rite which, until a few months ago, constituted a living tradition. We are referring to the Roman Catholic Mass. Yet, according to the latest information in Rome, there is a plan to obliterate that Mass by the end of the current year.*

Next, the signatories argued (as John Senior did) that the traditional Mass is foundational to, and inseparable from, western civilization:

> *We are not at this moment considering the religious or spiritual experience of millions of individuals. The rite in question, in its magnificent Latin text, has also inspired a host of priceless achievements in the arts ~not only mystical works, but works by poets, philosophers, musicians, architects, painters and sculptors in all countries and epochs. Thus, it belongs to universal culture as well as to churchmen and formal Christians.*

The implication is clear. If the "rite in question" has inspired the culture and lifted the human spirit in such a manner "in all countries and epochs", then what happens when it is distorted and diminished.

If western civilization exists for the Mass, then what happens when the Mass is changed? Consistently profaned? Modernized?

The letter concludes with both an appeal, and a filial warning, to the Holy Father:

> *The signatories of this appeal, which is entirely ecumenical and nonpolitical, have been drawn from every branch of modern culture in Europe and elsewhere. They wish to call to the attention of the Holy See, the appalling responsibility it would incur in the history of the human spirit were it to refuse to allow the Traditional Mass to survive...*

Cardinal Heenan delivered the letter to Pope Paul VI, resulting in the granting of the Latin Mass indult for England and Wales in November 1971.

What is sad today, nearly fifty years after the "reform" of the Roman Rite, is that many within the Church still do not see what John Senior and the signatories of the Agatha Christie letter so clearly recognized. History has proven them to be truly prophetic. We can view these last fifty years as our Babylonian exile. Our captivity, merited through pride and disobedience.

Surveying the ecclesial and cultural landscape near the end of his life, Senior held nothing back in his assessment:

> *The crisis is over; we have lost. This is no longer just a prediction, it is a simple observation: Rome has been desecrated. We are in the age of darkness. Triumphalist reactions are in vain. The modern world and the Church deserve the punishment that God is raining down on us.*

Despite this current punishment we cannot despair. In the end, we know Who is victorious. We do not, however, participate in this victory if we fail to reassert the fundamental connection between the Mass and western civilization.

The Mass must first be the foundation of the family before it can be the foundation of the culture. All of life must flow from Our Eucharistic Lord, present in our churches, on the altars, in the hands of our priests. The Social Kingship of Christ must once again be proclaimed as well.

We must also reject the nonsensical notion of the Mass as an ecumenical experiment. As a laboratory for innovation. As an expression of the secular instead of an encounter with the eternal. This must all be rejected. It is offensive and it is not Catholic.

Western civilization, or more accurately Christendom, exists for the Mass. We have seen the fruits of secularism, of rejecting this fundamental truth. We have seen both the culture and the Church teeter (and in some places fall) due to the loss of understanding of this foundational truth.

Even where the culture fails to grasp this notion, it is still true never the less.

In the end this is why so many fight for the liturgy, despite the scorn of some and the indifference of many. This truth compels us. Father John Zuhlsdorf (Fr. Z) likes to say, "Save the Liturgy, save the World." Indeed.

Bibliography

Ratzinger, Joseph Cardinal. *The Spirit of the Liturgy.* San Francisco: Ignatius Press, 2000.

Lang, Uwe Michael. *Turning Towards the Lord: Orientation in Liturgical Prayer.* San Francisco: Ignatius Press, 2004.

Schneider, Athanasius. *Dominus Est: It is the Lord.* Pine Beach: Newman House Press, 2008.

Spirago, Francis & Richard Clark SJ (Editor). *Catechism Explained: an Exhaustive Exposition of the Christian Religion.* New York, Cincinnati, Chicago: Benziger Brothers, 1899.

Cover Photo credit: Allison Girone

ABOUT THE AUTHOR

Brian Williams is a convert who entered the
Catholic Church in 2006. He is a graduate of Long
Beach State University with a B.A. in History.
Brian blogs on *Life, Liturgy and the Pursuit of Holiness* at
www.liturgyguy.com. He lives in Charlotte, North
Carolina with his wife and five children.